The Sara Poems

Roy Cameron

IRON
PRESS

First published 2007 by IRON Press
5 Marden Terrace, Cullercoats
Northumberland, NE30 4PD
tel/fax: +44 (0)191 253 1901
ironpress@blueyonder.co.uk
www.ironpress.co.uk

ISBN-13 978-0-9552450-3-9
ISBN-10 0-9552450-3-6

Printed by Field Print,
Boldon Colliery

FIRST EDITION

Typeset in Garamond

Cover artwork by David McConochie

IRON Press books are distributed by Central Books
and represented by Inpress Limited,
Northumberland House,
11 The Pavement, Pope's Lane,
Ealing, London W5 4NG
Tel: +44 (0)20 8832 7464
Fax: +44 (0)20 8832 7465
www.inpressbooks.co.uk

The Sara Poems

Acknowledgements

The poem *Promises* first appeared in Acumen no. 51

My heartfelt thanks to Patricia and William Oxley
for their help and advice.

Foreword

On the 21st of October, 2004, at the final hearing in the Newcastle Crown Court, the prosecuting counsel read out the following on my behalf:

I have been given the victim personal statement leaflet and the VPS scheme has been explained to me. What follows is what I wish to say in connection with this matter. I understand that what I say may be used in various ways and that it may be disclosed to the defence.

At the age of 23, just as her life was blossoming into full flower, my daughter was murdered. There are no words that can describe the shock, the pain and the loss I suffer. Sara was my only child and she meant everything to me. I am no longer a father. I will never be a grandfather. My life will never be the same.

For almost 4 years we have searched for her killer and I have had to work closely with the police whenever necessary. There has been no possibility of closure when every article written, every appeal for information spoken, has meant that the trauma had to be re-lived through - again and again.

The last remaining thing I have to do for my child is to ensure she has justice. Until this is done, there is no way I can "normalise" my life. But justice can be no consolation when nothing will bring her back and the rest of my life, as well as her mother's, has been blighted irrevocably.

God willing, one day we will have justice for Sara. God willing, the laws of our society will be upheld. But the void in my heart will never be filled.

On that day my daughter's killer was given a life sentence. And from that day on my life sentence will be to search for those words, words that hide below the horizon, that wait beyond the green hill, that are buried in the woods, that rest in the lines on the page.

Such words that I have found are all for her. For her eyes. For her voice.

R.C.

Contents

Gift

GIFT

As if a light comes on
when an angel
flicks a switch
and makes the universe shudder;

as if a prayer heard
in the constant thrum of rain
is building
an arch from our desire;

as if a sudden bright sky
comes dancing
across twilit furrowed
fields of snow;

like the smile
on the face of my child,
comes the wondrous
gift of love.

A PILE OF LOGS

There was a pile of freshly cut logs behind her, stacked high against
the wall. She had a backdrop of sunbursts that morning. Maybe it
was the pattern of irregular wheels, each rim jagging against the
other, interlocking spokes in a mirage of line and texture. Maybe it
was the glowing colour of the wood, so bright and clean in the sun
and maybe I can still recapture that glorious smell of pine, back
when I could trust my young and sensitive nose. But I remember that
moment so well.

She sat there on the ground with her back up against the logs, one
leg straight out in the grass, the other bent, propping the great ball of
her stomach. It was the spring of '76 and she was heavily pregnant, a
month or so to go. She was carrying our child, the epitome of a
country girl with her head swathed in a scarf, white rubber boots
shiny from the puddles, head tilted back with eyes closed to take in
the sun, the faintest of smiles playing on her lips. A soon to be
mother at rest with herself, at rest with child in her sun-warmed
womb and at rest with the world. At rest with a pile of logs.

A GIRL

It'll be a girl,
the taxi driver said
as he drove me to the clinic.
They always take their time.

He knew that I had waited all day,
had paced a sunlit floor,
had measured every lengthening shadow,
had pleaded with the phone.

Girls are best,
best for fathers, anyhow.
Twist you round their little finger.

Though I was the nervous one
he did all the talking
and in the end
I never did get the chance
to ask him how
he knew all this.

Girls are best,
best for fathers.

IN DELIVERY

Your father to be
spends his birthday
imitating a fish out of water.
They gift-wrapped me for you
in green plastic.

While unsleeping mother
has to endure the pain,
I doze off into the night.

Still you keep us in suspense,
long hours of floating
inside this shiny, sanitised bubble
with only mind-numbing musak
to welcome you.

You will have your own day…

All pink and blue-speckled
you slip out into the light
like a fat salmon
for the nurse to reel in.

So near I could touch you.
But you are slimy and blind,
you are new and afraid
and I am just a helpless, spellbound
father in delivery.

Till the air hits your lungs
and you shout, shout at the world,
with a mighty clarion call
that bursts the bubble
and the fears and the musak
are drowned in our tears of joy.
You are dangled before us,
our little prancing puppet–
and you are a girl.
You are a girl…

Now nestling in mother's arms,
all soft and serene and daughter of mine,
you already know what to do—
guzzling at the breast.

But what am I supposed to do
from this great distance,
now that I am left outside?

I'll just sit back and grin,
admire the scene before me and grin
and impatiently wait my turn
to take possession of our very own
little mistresspiece...

just to hold you in my arms.

LULLABY

Low and lovely
lullaby,
sleep now sweetheart
do not cry.
While you sleep
I'll be beside you,
soft in shadow
standing by.
You're the star
to still my sorrow
and light the sky.

Through the night
on wings you'll fly,
little angel
hushabye.
And each breath,
so deep the slumber,
brings a song
that you and I,
we will sing
will sing tomorrow
lullaby.

THE LONGEST SECONDS OF MY LIFE

She was only a baby and we were just fooling around, on a pleasant summer afternoon, playing down by the jetty, splashing in the water while the rest of the family looked on. I held her in my arms amid lots of screaming and laughter…

I took a sideways step and felt the bottom give way under me. To my horror we were suddenly being sucked into a black pit, spiralling down, deeper and deeper and I not knowing what was happening.

In my panic all I could do was kick furiously and with all my strength instinctively lift her high above my head. But the more I kicked it seemed the more I disturbed the soft thick muddy silt beneath us. We were corkscrewing down and I could not see or breathe.

It must have been only a few seconds before I felt her being lifted away from me. I kicked up from the mud and rose to the surface to see her gurgling in the arms of her grandfather, who, in turn, was roaring with laughter. Everybody seemed to think it was very funny. Long ago the shore by the jetty had been deepened to provide access for the boats. Everybody knew this, of course, except for the city-boy son-in-law!

SNAKE

Without a sound you suddenly
stopped dead in your tracks,
turned and jumped up into my arms.
And then I saw it,
right there before us,
a living coil of rope
twisting in the middle of the path,
the raised head mesmerising,
the pale jaws spread wide,
a hissing menace poised to strike.
Your mother must have walked right over it,
not seeing it from her height
but you, toddling along,
had looked it straight in the eyes.
The snake had woken from its hibernation,
was disturbed and clearly angered,
disorientated, perhaps blinded
in the spring sunlight
and with no intention
of just slithering off out of the way.
I knew its bite could kill
and carrying such precious cargo
I was not going to dispute the right of way—
enough room in the forest for us all.
So as you held me tight I circled
at a respectable distance
until we regained the path and could carry on.
But this time I would not put you down.

SARA'S FIRST DAY AT SCHOOL

Tell me something about your parents
the teacher asked each child,
so Sara piped up,
> *my Dad always asks my Mum,*
> *where are my underpants?*
> *and my Mum always answers,*
> *they're in the fridge.*

ADVENT CALENDAR

Not store bought, mass produced,
you made it all by yourself,
drew it, coloured it, cut and pasted it,
poured your very heart into every gift,
every tiny Christmas scene.

To me it was a magic lantern
for a wall of shadows.
It lit up the month.

I pinned it
between the building plans
and progress charts
and we grey old architects
took turns at morning coffee
to open a window
and let another little miracle
come shining in.

SIX HOUSES

Silent as sleep
but smiling in dreams;
six houses.

Wide-eyed with wonder,
windows of diamonds;
six houses.

Blue and then green
they are gliding,
orange and red, tiptoeing,
mulberry and yellow,
sleepwalking each one
up the steep white page
like ghosts in fancy dress
like floating balloons;
six houses.

Winter is holding its breath.
The smoke is frozen
in little girl ringlets.
Imagine the paths
where snow must be cleared
for the morning postman.

And like father like daughter,
she put a lopsided grin
on the merry old sun
as he strokes his whiskers.

LIGHTHOUSE

One great eye is shining,
shining out
in the darkest of storms.

9 years old,
she painted it
with flashing pastel strokes,
painted a prickly palm
standing defiantly
in a vast desert sea
while all around are
long black spears of rain
flung by a monstrous wind,
great waves splintering
the icy howling sky.

No bird could fly this fury,
no pirate run this main.
All sensible sea-serpents
safely tucked in bed.

I often wonder,
at this picture on my wall,
how a 9 year old
could find such elemental savagery?

But there it stands.
Her lighthouse
still on duty.

BAD DREAM

It was a dream I had,
only a bad dream…

A dream one night
from which I awoke
in a pool of sweat;
just the natural anxiety
any parent has for their child;
only a dream…

It is the middle of night.
We are standing together
on the heaving deck
of a rain-lashed ship that is
battling its way through the storm,
sea wolves all around, howling;
only a dream…

We hold tight to each other.
We have travelled
the seas many times
and we always laughed
at such crazy ghosts leaping at us;
only a dream…

Then you slip away
from the safety of my arms.
The wind lifts you
high into the air
and out, out, away from the ship.
I see you sucked up into the night
like a little bird tossed,
lost to the angry waves.
I see it over and over…

If I close my eyes as I write,
my fingers still on the keyboard,
I can see it still…

It was only a dream.

WE HAD PLANNED

that one day
you would marry
a nobleman–
Belgian or French, you said–
prince or count, we agreed–
with a large country estate;
as long as the house
had a wing
for father-in-law to live,
with at least one room
big enough
for a snooker table.

In An Instant

IN AN INSTANT

In an instant
all the world is changed–
what cannot happen
                    does.

Good Friday 2000–
I waited all day
for the phone to ring–
instead the doorbell–
                    the doorbell rang at midnight.

Instead the earth
was split in two
and the night sky
became a sea
            of blood.

It cannot be.
It doesn't happen.

> *There is a technical fault.*
> *Our engineers are working on it.*
> *We apologise for the inconvenience.*
> *Life will be resumed as soon as possible.*

It cannot be.
It cannot be.
Gone forever
in an instant.

The world stopped
when the bell rang–
but nobody else…
                    heard.

FATHER AS...

That is my daughter.
I remember my lips
must have moved–
father as ventriloquist's dummy.

And then I said, *thank you*,
as I turned away.
What a strange thing to say–
father as headless chicken.

How do you respond to someone
in such circumstances?
The coroner's assistant stood
motionless as an exhibit.

I walked out into the open air,
feeling like I was deserting you.
And then my mobile rang.
It was your mother.

WITHOUT

Without even realising,
I had started to run
and now I found
I could not stop.

The morning sun
sat on the horizon
in a sky as sharp as acid.
The beach unrolled
under my feet,
a smooth, endless carpet
of sand and windows.

I ran and I ran.
Down a corridor of adrenalin
I ran. I could not stop.
I sliced through air.

I ran through the forest
under its flickering canopy of green.
I ran with the snow
stinging in my eyes.
I could hear you calling me,
urging me on.

I ran and ran
till the sea ran out of land.
I ran and I ran.
I ran after you.

But I could not catch up.

BRUNO

When your mother
flew over
she brought Bruno with her
and placed him
in the coffin,
put him in your arms
just as she had done
so many times
when you had to be tucked in
with your soft,
cuddly old horse.

You called him Bruno.
You would not go to sleep
without him.
Bruno went through the fire
with you.

CLOSED HAND

If illness had taken you
I would have been there,
my hand in yours,
to tell you how much
I love you.

If you had been killed
in an accident
I could have forgiven
the unfeeling hand
that throws the dice.

But murder
was the icy hand
that gripped my heart,
that twisted and tightened
and would not let go.

It was the clenched fist,
the closed hand
of the senseless madman
and it will never
open.

EARSDON

In the field
outside the village
they planted the roses
on the spot
where you lay that night.

They are not easy to see
from the path
where the hedge
is thick and high.

Just an ordinary field
in a bleak and windswept land,
unploughed and overgrown,
it is a silent sheet of green.

Whenever the horses
are let out in the field
they come across
and sniff the blooms.

And when I visit,
the roses open like wounds;
lift their heads like comets;
shake defiant fists of blood;
their flames burn in the grass;
their petals of red acid
eat into my heart...

for on the spot
where you lay
they planted the roses,
they planted the roses
in a field
outside the village,
the village
of Earsdon.

THE CHAPEL DOOR

A pall of misty rain
covered everything.

A colourless rainbow
softened every edge
the day could offer,
eased away pain,
just for a moment,
like an ether
that leaves the eyes
unblinking.

The undertaker's car floated,
circled the chapel
like a bird about to land,
a wheeling black condor.

Women all around,
I did not see them.
Rain falling
did not touch me.

I stepped out
into a halo of faces,
blank, unsmiling,
open in the rain.

At their feet the flowers,
a garland of garlands,
as if we stood
on the rim of a crater
molten with fire.
I did not see its colour
but I felt its flame.

I stood with the students,
slowly turning,
round and round
this moment with them,
this moment in the rain,
when our world wept.

I looked at them all
one by one,
so young, so still
and so unquestioning,
my head slowly turning
until I saw
the chapel door.

My daughter was waiting.

RETURNING

That moment of falling
through the clouds
was like dropping through ice
into a bottomless lake,
feeling the swirling, twisting shock
of returning.

The open hand of Finland
once again held out below,
this old familiar counterpoint
of tidy field
and thick-trimmed forest
brought the music
I could not bear.
My weightless body fell
as snow in June.

I held your ashes
tight against my chest,
another desperate father
clinging to his child.

We were going home.

GOD DOES NOT EXPLAIN

God is with us,

the priest had said,
but God does not explain.

This was not an answer,
not words to ease the pain.

An old man has to ask,
his heart is broken—
but not his brain.

Such a simple question, God—
let me try again.

But there is nothing,
nothing to hold on to,
no end of this line.
I'm holding on to emptiness,
I'm holding on just fine.

God has His reasons,
God is not insane.

It's just that
God does not explain.

RETURN TO SENDER

I tried to parcel up my grief

like a package to be sent away.

I marked it *fragile; handle with care.*

No matter how I wrapped it

the pain kept dripping through.

I would post it if I could,

par avion

to the farthest corner of the world.

But who to send it to?

COMING TO THE CITY

We studied the map.
St. James Park;
the Haymarket;
a river laced with bridges;
a patchwork of universities;
that great loop of the Metro;
your next 3 years
spread out upon the table…

Now as I walk
those Geordie streets
my footsteps stumble
across your shadow,
my ears strain to catch
a pavement's toccata
and my voice is quickly gobbled
by a cold unfriendly wind.
Now as I speak my lines
and faces fly before me
I am twisted into granite.
Now as the evening sun
sets over the rooftops
the Tyne slashes its nets
like a dying warrior wields
his sword of whetted steel.
Now as queue-jumping pigeons
jostle to paint the bridge,
laying the patina of our days,
I wait and watch the dusk
as it slowly falls.

We studied the map.
Our fingers went shopping
along Northumberland Street,
clutching our hopes and promises,
coming to the city.

Promises

FOR SARA

In the still of morning
a raindrop falls
and makes the forest tremble...

you were to me like a brook,
come to warm my frosty field,
wearing a tiara of kisses...

a supple little stream, smiling,
basking in sunlight
slip-sliding down the valley...

growing, flowing, river like a mirror
silver snaking through
the muddy delta of my heart...

going away, too soon, away
to the deep and star wise sea,
to be held forever in its dream...

asleep, asleep my love, out there
on the pillows of the ocean,
out there on the far side of my night.

NAME DAY

I cannot give you
a rose on this day
so I write it instead–

write it so red–
each sunset will seem
as pale as a ghost–

write it so bright–
the eyes will go blind
reading these lines–

write it so full–
a heart cannot hold
or the world imagine.

GRADUATION 28th JUNE 2001

The audience rose to its feet
when her name was called.
I stepped out from the line
of gowned young men and women
and started to cross the boards.
A great wave of emotion seemed
to swell up through the auditorium
and come crashing onto the stage.

I felt the applause wash over me.

I felt the weightlessness of an astronaut
on his first walk in outer space. I knew his fear.
I watched as my hand, stretched out
to greet the Chancellor, became a bridge
spanning the vast distance
to where he stood mouthing words at me
through the sonic boom.

And in the middle of all this clamour
I could hear the small still voice
of someone who should have been there,
someone who had already left the theatre
taking with her a proud-parent heart,
leaving behind only this hapless novice
who was frozen with stage fright,
who was caught in the arc lights,
the understudy standing there
in her place.

TWO YEARS

Two years dead...
I have tailored my days
like a suit.

Time does not pass...
it just spreads out
like a river overflowing...

see, there is the boat,
there she sits rowing.

Time does not heal...
it picks at the dreams
where blood can't congeal...

time does not mend...
it just keeps stitching
at the seams.

MOONSEARCH

Like children
in a starry playground
just a blink away,
on a high field
sprinkled with daisies
we play hide and seek.

I have to be the one
to close my eyes
and count to ten.
Slowly.

Slowly, so slowly
all the rest of my days,
while you run and hide
behind the moon's
shiny shield,
among the shadows
of the night.

No matter how hard I count,
I cannot follow.
The distance is too great.

You win, you win.
I am hopeless at this game.
Come out, come out,
wherever you are!

And if you tire of waiting
and come out,
you will find me cheating,
as always,
like a blind man
counting with his eyes open,
searching in the mountains
of the moon.

PROMISES

While you are gone
I promise to dust your constellations
and water all the planets
on your window sill.
I will answer all their messages.

I promise to take your laughter
out for its walk each day,
up high along the cliff path
and share it with the hedge sparrows.

And when we grow tired
I can rest our weary bones
in the Armchair Rock
and cut you a slice
of Sugarloaf Hill.

We could lay back and listen
to the vapour trails
strung out across the sky,
or instruct the dolphins
in their aerobics class.

And as the daylight fades
I promise to sit with you,
close by the water's edge
and tell the breeze your bedtime story.
Then, when the sea drops off to sleep,
I will get up and gently tuck
the evening in
and kiss you on the cheek.

FLOWERS

Not for me, for my daughter. I particularly favour lilies with their head bowed trumpet-like looks—I hear Miles playing something plaintive and soulful, muted and melancholic. I have never been a flower person but now there has to be a constant presence of fresh-cut flowers. Lilies. Tulips in the spring. Or roses, they last well and hardly ever seem to wither but age gracefully, as if they understand the beauty of time, how to grow old in grace. The love and the dignity of a rose—a red, red rose.

And I have never been a collector of photographs either. Endlessly repetitive snaps of holidays or weddings bore me to tears, but now pictures have been framed and stand there on my low table; my little girl meeting the Finnish president at the age of two, my sporting daughter rowing the boat for me on our day out in Durham, the young woman sitting thoughtfully in her mother's kitchen in Helsinki, the large gold-framed one they gave me from the memorial service. On the wall is the star chart and her posthumous diploma from the university – *degree aegrotat of Bachelor of Science in Sport Management* : *European*. In the front, the statuette she won racing in Washington. I put them all there but I can hardly bear to look at them.

Except, of course, the flowers. These I can look at all the time. I arrange them between the picture frames to soften this composition of rigid rectangles. They symbolise the love, remembrance and all the other things that men bring women flowers for, I guess. I have given flowers to a fair share of women in my life, but never to my daughter when she was alive, she would have thought that just plain silly. Do fathers give their daughters flowers? Maybe in some cultures, I don't know.

The single candle is the centrepiece. I light it each and every evening I am home, and it burns until it's time for bed. Sometimes I run out of matches if I forget to buy a new box. That makes me feel bad and the evening is wretched. I feel I am letting her down. I will burn a candle for her every night for the rest of my life. It's not much, I know, but it's all I can do.

THE BEST YEARS

were the years
of watching my daughter grow,
an adventure in every step,
sunlight in every laugh;
the posy of wild flowers
mother picked for her
and the little dress
of vibrant colours;
a quarter of a century
on a merry-go-round
that goes on whirling,
whirling inside my head.

VELKUA

The end of my day…
to smell again the pines
where so many times
the sun would be sinking
like a Roman candle
down among the trees.

The end of my day…
to hear again the echo
of children's laughter
across the polished water
where fish went dancing
with the dragonflies.

The crooked jetty
would point its bony finger
at the malingering moon.
Its boards would creak
beneath our feet
and announce our arrival
so the courteous sea
could hold the mirror
for its guests.

The end of my day…
to float again in that silver sky
high above the world,
put its music in your voice
and conjure in your eyes
that precious summer light.

IN COURT

How do you look at the man who has murdered your child?
Her mother told me later that when she first saw his face in the
newspaper she was violently sick. I was to see him paraded
before me in court.

I had resolved to look straight at his face, to stare unflinchingly
at him no matter whether he turned to me or not, deliberately
to detach myself from the proceedings so that I could get
through them. In order to avoid thinking about what he had
done, I would try to analyse his face, to read his body language
as if I might be researching data for some future project.

There was a small cage-like structure at the side of the court.
He came in, flanked on either side by a police officer. I hardly
noticed them, I gave him my total concentration. He stood,
looking straight at the magistrate, barely moving a muscle, only
reacting to confirm his name.

I was nevertheless taken aback at first by how old he appeared:
29, he looked to me more like 40. Shaven-headed, surprisingly
small, but probably wiry and strong. I told myself I must not
think about what he has done. I just stared at his profile, his
nose, his cheekbones. I was a few feet away. Our eyes did not
meet. And then he was gone.

Tapped on the shoulder, I had to turn, because I was to be the
first to leave the courtroom. I knew, of course, that all eyes
would be on me and so I did my best to keep my head held
high as I made for the door. I saw nothing else and nobody
else. My lips were tightly shut and I breathed deeply through
my nostrils as I felt I was beginning to hyperventilate. Hold it,
hold it, keep yourself together, walk down this tunnel of
nightmare, through the door, across the hall, along the corridor,
down the stairs until, finally, out from the building and into the
fresh air.

Fresh air on my face. Sun in my eyes, blinding. And pain, pain
in my heart from having to go on living.

RAVEN

At the point where the cliff
climbs high above the sea
a raven was waiting,
perched on his fencepost.
He must have sensed my approach
though he didn't even shuffle his feet.
Instead his one eye glistened,
reflecting the slanting sunlight
like a stop-sign which I was to obey.
I stood to attention,
admired the coat of coal-black sheen
and was duly impressed
by his military demeanour.
The soft wind that ruffled
each feather on his back
ruffled each hair on my head
and became the interpreter
for this confrontation–
sentry at the gate,
intruder from below–
wordlessly debating our next move.
No giving of ground,
heads held high,
attentive to the wind's translations,
motionless as mourners
in the centre circle,
though only one of us
was suitably dressed.
Our stand-off silence
was observed impeccably
until the circle began to spin,
spin, spin around his pedestal
and it seemed
that earth and sky were melting,
blurring, spinning on a potter's wheel
into a new beginning
for man and bird.

NEW MOON

There is a new moon tonight,
conjured in a way, I like to think,
that is just for you and me.

The evening has put on
a cloud dappled shirt, has dressed
in shades of such soft glow,
in shine of such serenity
no star dares to interfere. Not yet.

But there it is,
like a majestic, magic button
sewn on a suit of velvet,
a big, black, plump old fellow
lording it up there
and scratching his belly,
girdled as it is
with a precisely stitched
crescent sash of gold
as thin as a grin, so bright
I expect the cow to jump
at any moment.

The world ignores
such precious moments
as it rushes home from work.
But our hearts are still
and still in wonder, this evening,
under this new moon.

It is good
to look up together
and see the old man
is still swinging.

LANDSCAPE IN PINK, EASTER 2005

Five years have passed and I
see the lambs are wearing
pink this season,
busy polka dotting the hillsides.

Is this a trick of the light,
a rusting on the retinas
that comes with the advancing age
of my bloodshot Devon eyes?

Or are these lambs thus preserved
and pickled at birth?
Did they frolic too much in the mud,
stay out in the rain at sunset?

From the bottom of his field
a retired old workhorse
looks up dismayed by it all
and shakes his weary head at me.

Winter's dirge was played
to dull my senses
so the world might pass me by,
but now the bleat of spring

has come to stir me
and open my eyes once more.
On a bittersweet canvas—
brushstrokes of falling pink petals.

GINGILOS

Lefka Ori.
The mountains wore
their long white robes
and stood in line
to welcome us.

They showed us the wisdom
and eloquence of their old stones
well scarred in syllables
of fire and fissure.
They spoke with the silence
of a searching heart.

Eagle eyes
watched us climb
throughout the day.

To reach the saddle was hard,
but harder still
that last steep wall
of clambering pain,
before the Mediterranean
could wrap its misty arms
around us.

A simple tablet of slate.

We left your name
on Gingilos
for the gods
to anoint with their burning
torch of sun
and bless
with their eternal kiss
of snow,
while the world below
sleeps on.

LULLABYE

There is no music
for the song
I never thought to write.
Your sleep that came
too soon has left me
silenced in the night.

So now the stone
must sing your name
and mountain cradle high.
On the other side
of sunset there is
one last lullaby.

ALCHEMY

Open my eyes, surprise,
I see sunlight on dew
has strung for you
a necklace from these tears.

I am now brave as a wave
riding in on the foam,
bringing you home
from a long night's vigil.

Our song fills the air, I dare
to go on living,
forgiving
the dark clouds of morning,

spinning the dreams, it seems,
in the palm of my hand,
to understand
how grief turns to joy.

AFTERWORD

She is always with me.

I think of her,
hold on to her,
fill the hills
and the hollows
of each day with her.

Her absence all around
walks with me
from room to room.

Every morning I wake
to the news of her death.
Daily the bulletins tell me
she is dead and I am
slowly dying with her.

In this house of struggle
she has become the mortar
that keeps each brick
from crumbling to a pile of dust.

One day I must step outside.
Before I go
I will switch off the light
and pin all the suffering
inside the door…

LAST WILL AND TESTAMENT

...and when I go,
no more to grieve
or possessions to leave,
let it stay behind–
all I ever needed to own
the love of my child
and her love for me,
that was ours alone,
conjoined, entwined,
more durable than stone,

that will always live on
though we both are gone.

Roy Cameron

Roy Cameron was born and grew up in London, working there as an architect until his move to Finland in 1973. His daughter Sara was born in Helsinki in 1976 and both were granted dual nationality. Roy returned to England in 1977 and now lives in Devon. Sara had spent two years at the University of Northumbria in Newcastle.